ANIMAL BABIES

BABY SEALS

by Jennifer Boothroyd

Consultant: Beth Gambro
Reading Specialist, Yorkville, Illinois

BEARPORT PUBLISHING

Minneapolis, Minnesota

Teaching Tips

Before Reading

- Look at the cover of the book. Discuss the picture and the title.
- Ask readers to brainstorm a list of what they already know about seals. What can they expect to see in this book?
- Go on a picture walk, looking through the pictures to discuss vocabulary and make predictions about the text.

During Reading

- Read for purpose. Encourage readers to think about seals and the animal life cycle as they are reading.
- If readers encounter an unknown word, ask them to look at the sounds in the word. Then, ask them to look at the rest of the page. Are there any clues to help them understand?

After Reading

- Encourage readers to pick a buddy and reread the book together.
- Ask readers to name three things that seals do between the time they are born and when they are ready to have babies. Go back and find the pages that tell about these things.
- Ask readers to write a sentence and draw a picture of something that they learned about seals.

Credits:
Cover and title page; © Michel VIARD/iStock; 3, © Vladimir Melnik/Shutterstock; 5, © All Canada Photos/Alamy Stock Photo; 6, © Rinus Baak/Dreamstime; 7, © Kevin Schafer/Getty Images; 9, © Kevin Schafer/Alamy Stock Photo; 10, © Sunvincible/iStock; 12-13, © Nature Picture Library/Alamy Stock Photo; 15, © COULANGES/Shutterstock; 16, © Barcroft/Getty Images; 18-19, © Dolores M. Harvey/Shutterstock; 21, © AleksandrN/Shutterstock; 22, © Vladimir Melnik/Shutterstock; 23BL, © Vladimir Melnik/Shutterstock; 23BM, © Enrique Aguirre/Shutterstock; 23BR, © Rinus Baak/Dreamstime; 23TL, © Saperlo/Alamy Stock Photo; 23TR, © Joe Raedle/Getty Images

Library of Congress Cataloging-in-Publication Data

Names: Boothroyd, Jennifer, 1972– author.
Title: Baby seals / Jennifer Boothroyd.
Description: Bearcub books. | Minneapolis : Bearport Publishing Company,
[2021] | Series: Animal babies | Includes bibliographical references and
index.
Identifiers: LCCN 2020038303 (print) | LCCN 2020038304 (ebook) | ISBN
9781647474737 (library binding) | ISBN 9781647474812 (paperback) | ISBN
9781647474898 (ebook)
Subjects: LCSH: Seals (Animals)—Infancy—Juvenile literature.
Classification: LCC QL737.P64 B663 2021 (print) | LCC QL737 .P64 (ebook) |
DDC 599.7913/92—dc23
LC record available at https://lccn.loc.gov/2020038303
LC ebook record available at https://lccn.loc.gov/2020038304

For more information, write to Bearport Publishing, 5357 Penn Avenue South, Minneapolis, MN 55419.

Printed in the United States of America.

Contents

It's a Baby Seal!

Brrr!

This baby was born on ice.

But the little seal has **thick** yellow fur.

It keeps the **newborn** warm.

A baby seal is called a **pup**.

It is the size of a two-year-old child.

There are many kinds of seals.

This is a harp seal.

The pup drinks milk from its mother's body.

Slurp!

The milk helps the baby seal grow.

In a couple of days, the little seal changes color.

Its fur is now fluffy and white.

The pup is the same color as snow.

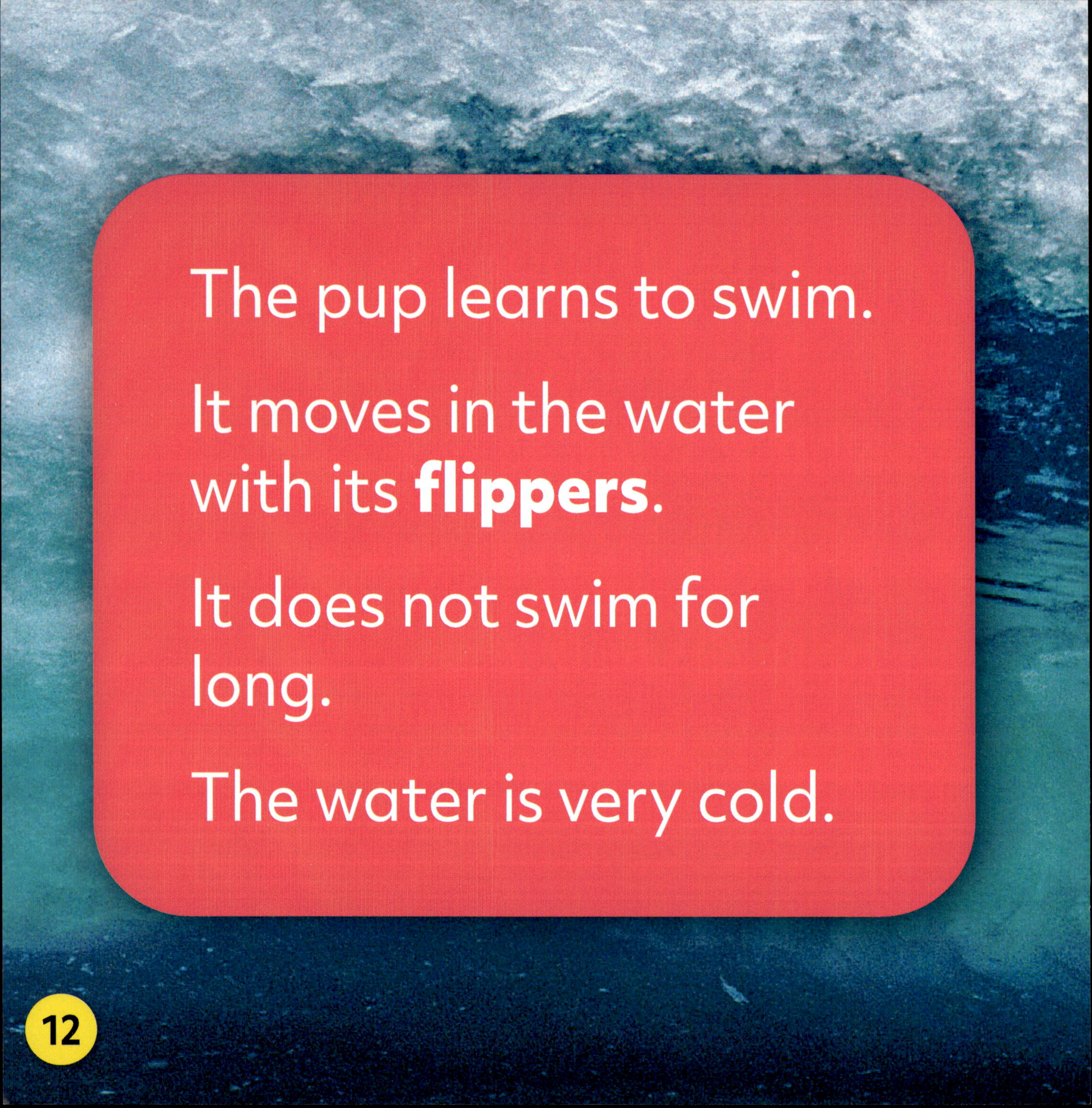

The pup learns to swim.

It moves in the water with its **flippers**.

It does not swim for long.

The water is very cold.

The pup grows a lot in the first two weeks.

Then, its mother leaves.

The baby lives alone on the ice.

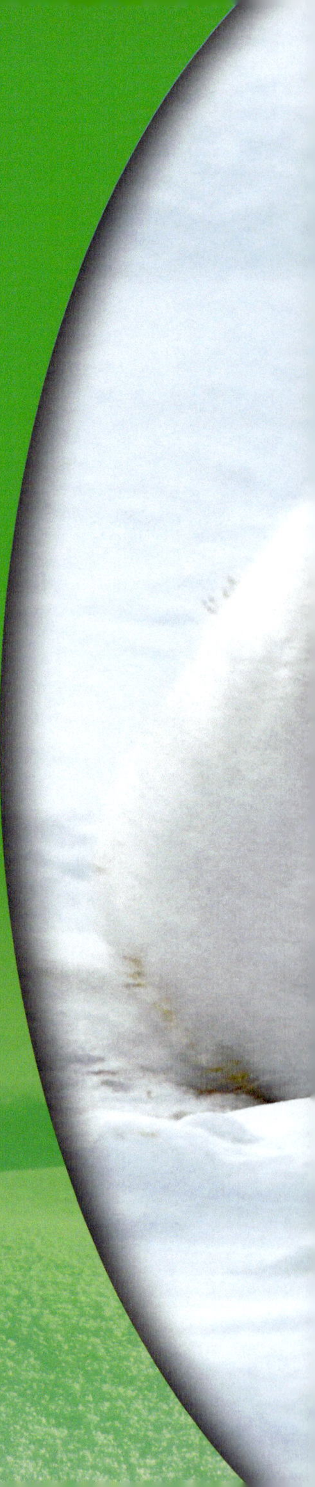

A month later, the pup has new fur.

It is gray.

Look at those spots!

This new fur will help the seal swim faster.

The seal is very **hungry**.

It has not eaten since its mother left.

It will dive into the water to find food.

Munch!

The baby keeps growing.

When the seal is four years old, it is an adult.

It can have a pup of its own.

The Baby's Body

Glossary

flippers the body parts that help some animals swim

hungry feeling the need for food

newborn just born

pup a baby seal

thick lots of something very close together

Index

Read More

Nilsen, Genevieve. *Harp Seal Pups (Polar Babies).* Minneapolis: Jump!, 2020.

Pettiford, Rebecca. *Harp Seals (Blastoff! Readers.* Animals of the Arctic). Minneapolis: Bellwether Media, 2019.

Learn More Online

1. Go to **www.factsurfer.com**
2. Enter "**Baby Seals**" into the search box.
3. Click on the cover of this book to see a list of websites.

About the Author

Jennifer Boothroyd enjoys visiting museums and nature centers.